CARTON GARDENING MANUAL

DEFINITE DIRECTIONS ON GROWING VEGETABLES IN CONTAINERS

ANDY COBELL

Table of Contents

CHAPTER ONE

CARTON GARDENING

Growing Vegetables in Containers: A Primer

Even if you don't have a yard, you can still grow vegetables successfully in containers. Consider gardening in containers if your available gardening space is limited to a balcony, roof, or other elevated platform.

Reasons YOU Ought to Attempt Container Gardening

Growing your own food doesn't have to be limited to those with access to a large plot of land or raised beds. Do you wish you had better command over your growing conditions and encountered fewer weeds? Growing plants in containers allows you to make the most of your gardening space and reduces the time you spend tending to them.

Methods for Growing Vegetables in Containers

How and Where to Set Up Your Container Garden

A container garden's greatest asset is its portability. Growing plants in containers lets you make the most of any plot of land, even if it's just a couple of pots on the edge of your driveway or a sliver of your balcony.

Think about things like sun exposure, water availability, and wind protection just as you would for a traditional garden bed when deciding where to put your containers.

Place your pots in a spot that gets at least six hours of sunlight a day if you want the most out of your vegetable garden (i.e., 6 to 8 hours of sunlight per day). Fruiting plants like tomatoes, peppers, squash, and eggplant need full sun, but leafy greens like lettuce and spinach can thrive with only 3–5 hours per day. The sunniest and warmest locations are those facing south and west, while the north and east are in constant shadow.

Plant containers should be placed where you can easily access them with a hose for watering. There's nothing worse than having to lug a gardening can across your yard a dozen times every morning and again in the evening to water your container garden, as containers typically require more water than standard in-ground gardens. To save time and energy, it's helpful to have water nearby that you can quickly access.

Assuring that containers are shielded from the wind reduces the rate at which their contents dry out and eliminates the risk of them being knocked over by the wind. Plants and containers can become top-heavy over the course of the season, making them more likely to topple over in windy conditions. Store containers indoors or make other preparations for their safety (e.g., with cinderblocks, stones, or ropes).

Finally, consider the various microclimates that can be found on your land. A microclimate is a localized area whose weather is significantly different from the surrounding environment. A potted plant set on a driveway, for instance, would benefit from the asphalt's ability to retain heat for longer than a patch of grass. There's a chance this will speed up the rate at which the pots dry out, but plants could benefit from the warmer soil if this is the case.

CHAPTER TWO

Find the Right Container for Your Needs

As expected, the first step in successful container gardening is deciding on a suitable container. Almost anything that can hold soil can be used as a garden container, from plastic pots and cinderblocks to whiskey barrels and wheelbarrows. However, there are three crucial factors to consider when selecting a container for a productive vegetable garden in a container:

1. Sewerage

A drainage hole or other means of water escape from a container is required. Soil that becomes waterlogged encourages the growth of bacteria and fungi, which reduce plant growth and ultimately kill them. It's also important to consider your local climate: gardeners in arid regions may want to select containers that hold more water, while those in humid regions may prefer containers with better air circulation.

2. Size

In general, the more space you can offer your plants' roots, the better they will grow. Larger vegetables, especially those with thicker skins, will need more space than the standard 12 inches of soil. Plants with deep roots, such as tomatoes and squash, require a 5-gallon container, while plants with shallow roots, like lettuce and greens, can be grown in smaller containers.

Keep in mind that larger containers are going to be heavier and harder to move, and might not be suitable for a place like a balcony. Conversely, small containers have the benefits of portability and adaptability, but they also dry out more quickly and require more maintenance on hot days.

3. the stuff

The material the container is made of is the final critical factor. There is a wide variety of containers available today, each with its own set of advantages and disadvantages. Some of the most widely used types of packaging are as follows:

One of the most common materials for planters is plastic because of the wide variety of styles available. Most other materials are more expensive than plastic pots, which are typically the least expensive option. They can be used for multiple gardening seasons, are simple to clean, and weigh very little. If you're growing food, it's important to use food-grade plastic containers so that no chemicals seep into the soil.

- Ceramic (terra cotta): Ceramic pots are also very common. They are more attractive than plastic pots, but much more cumbersome to move around, especially when they are loaded down with soil. Glazed ceramic pots are better at retaining moisture than their unglazed counterparts, but both types are available. Because clay is porous, air and water can circulate to some extent within a ceramic container. Soil is protected from becoming too wet, but (unglazed) clay pots allow soil to dry out more quickly than plastic ones. More so, empty ceramic pots and store them in a dry, warm place for the winter to prevent them from cracking from the cold.

Fabric: Fabric planters have increased in popularity in recent years because of their portability and airiness. They're typically equipped with handles, too, so you can carry them with ease.

Also, they are simple to clean and reuse. The fabric's porosity facilitates air and water circulation, which in turn encourages the development of fibrous root systems that are more adept at absorbing water and nutrients. It's important to remember to water your plants regularly in fabric pots because they dry out quickly.

It's worth repeating that practically anything serves as a suitable container, so use your imagination! Herbs, cherry tomatoes, and strawberries grown at eye level in hanging baskets are efficient uses of vertical space and are easily tended and harvested. Grow your own food in anything from whiskey barrels (even a wooden half-barrel can produce a surprising amount of food) to buckets, baskets, boxes, bath and other tubs, window boxes, and troughs. Make sure it has holes in the bottom for drainage and is a manageable size.

If you need help deciding which container is best for your needs, check out the video down below:

Canister Soil

A healthy soil is essential for growing healthy plants. To promote strong root development and a bountiful harvest, container-grown plants require optimal conditions for nutrition, oxygenation, and drainage.

The garden shouldn't be used as a soil source. In most cases, garden soils are too heavy, are prone to becoming waterlogged and compacted, and are a breeding ground for pests and diseases. You should instead use a container-specific "soilless" potting mix. In addition to being lightweight and draining quickly, it should also be disease and pest free.

Peat (or coconut coir), perlite, and vermiculite are the main components of most soilless potting mixes. Other ingredients, such as ground limestone and granulated fertilizers, are sometimes included. How to make your own soilless mix at home is detailed here.

Got any compost? With its high nutrient content and ability to aerate the growing medium, humus is a fantastic addition to any container mix. Learn all about composting by reading this article!

CHAPTER THREE

Useful Information Regarding Water Storage Containers

Containers dry out faster than ground-level gardens or raised beds because they receive less protection from the elements. Many plants grown in containers require watering as often as twice a day, especially during the hottest days of summer.

It is possible to water plants in containers with a hose, a watering can, or a drip irrigation system. Pick a strategy that works well with the space you have available in your garden.

Watering Tips and Tricks:

Start your day off with some H2O. (or as early as possible). Watering container plants first thing in the morning helps them get the most out of the moisture throughout the day. Plants can survive the hottest part of the day with the help of an early morning watering. This helps to prevent the spread of disease by making sure their leaves are completely dry before nightfall.

Water thoroughly. Watering plants by spraying the soil's surface is insufficient because plants require water at their roots. Be sure to thoroughly and deeply water your plants, especially those in containers, so that the moisture can penetrate all the way to the roots. It's important to water until the soil is soggy and water drains out of the bottom of the container. You could also water from below: Get a tray, fill it with water, and set it under the pot. This drainage hole will allow water to seep into the soil, where it can be absorbed (s). To dispose of the remaining water in the tray, repeat the process until it is no longer necessary to do so.

Don't over-water your plants! It may seem counterintuitive, but it's actually worse to water a plant frequently with a small amount of water than to water it infrequently with a large amount of water. In contrast to infrequent deep watering, which encourages deeper, healthier roots to form, frequent shallow watering leads to weak, shallow root development in plants. Don't be afraid to let the soil dry out slightly between deep waterings; most plants can tolerate and even benefit from this.

The size of the pot and the expected weather are also important considerations. Much more frequent watering will be required for smaller containers because they will dry out much faster. Expect to water more frequently during heat waves because hot, sunny days are inherently more drying than cool, cloudy days. The frequency of watering can be estimated by observing the rate at which the soil in your containers dries out and the subsequent response of your plants.

A good way to ensure that plants in containers stay cool and moist during the hot summer months is to double-pot them: Plants can be kept indoors by nesting a smaller pot inside a larger one and filling the void with sphagnum moss or crumpled newspaper. Don't forget to water the filler between the pots when you water the plant. Be wary of double-potted plants; the extra layer provides a nice hiding place for pests, so check on them frequently.

Containerized Fertilization

Nutrients are washed out of storage containers as water moves through them rapidly. For the most part, this is beneficial because it removes salts from the soil. This, however, means that container plants require more frequent feedings than those grown in the ground to replace the nutrients lost during watering.

At the beginning of the gardening season, it is best to add a slow-release fertilizer to your potting mix. You can either incorporate the fertilizer into the potting mix at the time of planting, or apply it as a top-dressing to the soil immediately after planting. Your plants will benefit from the extra boost in development this provides.

While they're actively growing, flowering, and fruiting, use a liquid fertilizer to feed container plants at least twice a month, following the instructions on the label. To determine if additional fertilizer is required, testing the soil is always recommended. Container soil can also benefit from the occasional addition of fish emulsion or compost, both of which are rich in trace elements.

Soil amendments such as liquid seaweed, fish emulsion, or manure tea can be used to sustain the growth of vegetable plants. In this article, you will learn how to fertilize container plants.

Container Plant Stability Support

We're not saying you can't have a little friendly banter with your plants, but in this case, we're talking about actual assistance. Use trellises, stakes, netting, twine, or cages to provide support for tall or climbing vegetables. Here's a guide to constructing your very own wooden trellis or supports.

If you want to grow pole beans or snap peas, a teepee made of bamboo stakes is a good way to do it. Trained cucumber vines climbing a nylon mesh fence produce straight, hanging fruit. Installing supports at planting time prevents later problems with the plants' roots and stems.

How well do various vegetables thrive when planted in pots?

There are some vegetables that do better than others when grown in containers. Plants that are easily transplanted make excellent candidates for container gardening because they adapt quickly to their new surroundings. You can get transplants from nurseries close to you or start them in your own greenhouse.

Choose "dwarf" or "container" vegetable varieties because they tend to remain compact and thrive in confined spaces. You can find vegetable varieties developed for growing in containers in many seed catalogs. Pick "bush" or "determinate" varieties of tomatoes, for example, because they will stay a manageable size in a pot even as they grow.

Edible flowers like nasturtiums, calendula, and signet marigolds not only look pretty in window boxes, but they also bring a splash of color to the dinner table.

Planting both short- and tall-stemmed plants in the same pot will help you make the most of the available space and increase your yield. Climbers eagerly scale a trellis, with smaller plants clustered at their feet.

You won't have to spend much time weeding because there will be nowhere for weeds to take root, and in the heat of summer, low-growing plants (such as leafy greens) can benefit from the shade cast by the taller ones.

Plants with different maturation times should be planted together; for example, lettuce and radishes should be planted alongside tomatoes and broccoli. Here you can get information on how to grow salad greens in containers.

Plants with similar water and light requirements should be grown together; for example, pole beans, radishes, and lettuce; bush beans, tomatoes, basil, and onions; and peas and carrots.

CHAPTER FOUR

Finally, here are some vegetables that would do well in containers, along with some suggestions for what size and type of containers you should use:

Put the beans in a snap

5-gallon window box as a holding container

Blue Lake bush, Romano bush, and tender crop bush are all types of this plant.

Broccoli

One plant per 5 gallon pot, or three plants per 15-gallon tub.

'DeCicco,' 'Green Comet,' and other varieties.

Carrots

Plant in a 12-inch-deep window box, preferably a 5-gallon one.

Types include the "Danvers Half Long," "Short 'n Sweet," and the "Tiny Sweet."

Cucumbers

One plant per one gallon container.

Plants of the 'Patio Pik,' 'Pot Luck,' and 'Spacemaster' varieties

Eggplant

5-gallon pots, one plant per container

Black Beauty, Ichiban, and Slim Jim are all varieties.

Lettuce

5-gallon window box as a holding container

Types include the "Ruby" and "Salad Bowl."

Onions

5-gallon window box as a holding container

White Sweet Spanish and Yellow Sweet Spanish are two examples of these types.

Peppers

One plant per three-gallon pot, or five plants per 15-gallon tub.

You can choose from "Cayenne," "Long Red," "Sweet Banana," "Wonder," and "Yolo."

Radishes

5-gallon window box as a holding container

The 'Cherry Belle' and 'Icicle' varieties are available.

Tomatoes

5-gallon pots, one plant per container

Early Girl, Patio, Small Fry, Sweet 100, and Tiny Tim are some of the varieties available.

www.ingramcontent.com/pod-product-compliance
Lightning Source LLC
LaVergne TN
LVHW010509160826
845677LV00012B/2748
* 9 7 9 8 8 4 7 0 7 5 2 1 3 *